MIMICRY AND CAMOUFLAGE IN NATURE

Ruth Soffer

DOVER PUBLICATIONS, INC.
Mineola, New York

Bibliographical Note

Mimicry and Camouflage in Nature is a new work, first published by Dover Publications, Inc., in 2002.

DOVER *Pictorial Archive* SERIES

International Standard Book Number: 0-486-41867-7

Manufactured in the United States of America
Dover Publications, Inc., 31 East 2nd Street, Mineola, N.Y. 11501

INTRODUCTION

Among the many fascinating aspects of the evolution of countless species of living beings are the elements of camouflage and mimicry. In this book, nature artist Ruth Soffer introduces a wide range of animals that increase their chances of capturing prey and avoiding predators by making themselves "invisible" in their surroundings, or by disguising themselves as different—usually dangerous—creatures.

Animals that use mimicry or camouflage to live longer and to reproduce successfully include creatures of the land, air, and water: mammals, birds, amphibians, reptiles, insects, arthropods, and fish. Such creatures are found on each continent, in all climates, and in every kind of habitat, from coral reef to rain forest to grassland to desert. Also included in this selection of masqueraders is a flower that resembles a bee, in both appearance and fragrance!

From the hefty polar bear to tiny hawkfish and tree frogs, from the speedy cheetah to the lumbering hermit crab, from the well-known chameleon to the obscure cuttlefish, these creatures of camouflage and masters of mimicry will surprise you with their unusual combinations of color, pattern, and form. Always impressive (leaf katydids, walkingstick insects, the Thorn-Mimic Tree Hopper), sometimes truly amazing (for example, the recently discovered Mimic Octopus), the animals portrayed in 28 scenes are special representatives of the wonders of nature.

INDEX OF COMMON NAMES

INDEX OF SCIENTIFIC NAMES

The **Polar Bear** (*Ursus maritimus*) lives along the coasts of the Arctic Ocean, where its white fur camouflages it against the background of snow and ice. Both when it is hunting (ringed seals are the main food of polar bears) and when it is trying to avoid hunters (humans are the main predators of polar bears, which rarely are killed by other animals) this large meat-eater uses the landscape cleverly to hide its bulk. Polar bears usually move relatively slowly on land, being insulated by lots of fat, but they are strong swimmers and can stay underwater for more than a minute.

1

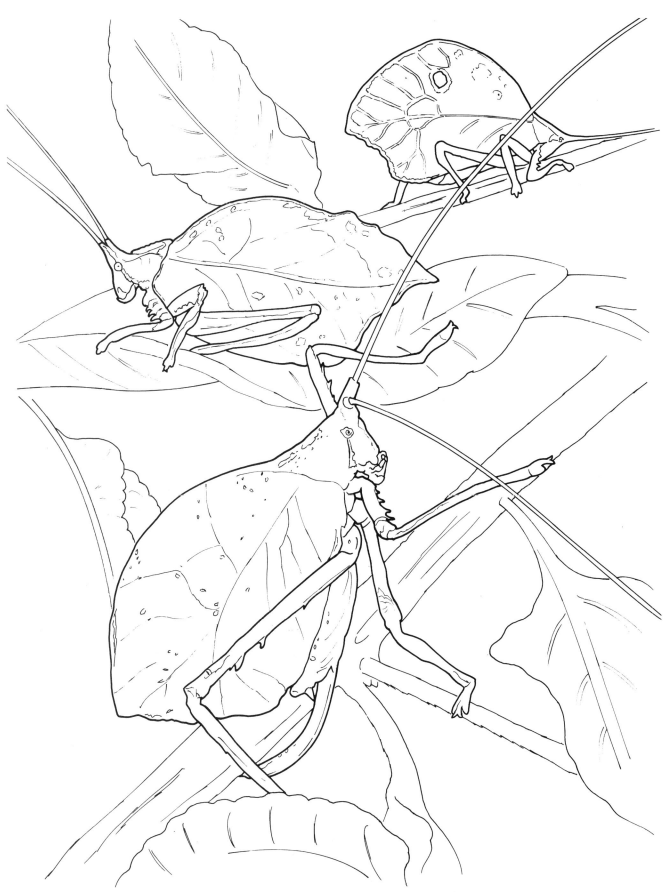

Numerous species of leaf katydids, long-horned grasshoppers in the subfamily Pseudophyllinae, live on the leaf-covered floor of rain forests and in the understory of rain-forest trees on several continents and islands. All are green, or green and brown, in color. The adults of many species in the Amazon rain forest resemble dead leaves, or partially eaten leaves, which stops potential predators (monkeys, spiders, and birds) from eating these insects. The leaf katydids feed on the leaves among which they live. In Australia, *Mastigaphoides* species are common.

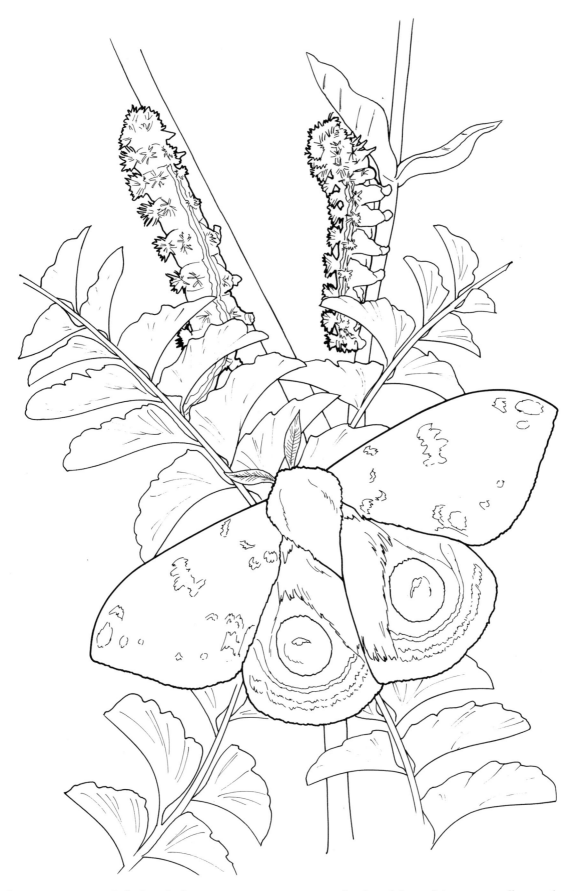

The male *Automeris io* moth flashes the large "eyes" on its hind wings to frighten away any bird that touches it with its beak. Startled birds fear that the "eyes" belong to a large predator. The sharp spines of the caterpillars (two are shown on the plant stems) are mildly poisonous. The background color of the male's wings is yellow, with wide rusty orange bands along the inner edges of the hind wings. The colors of the caterpillar are green, pink, and white. Both the caterpillar and the moth feed on a variety of plants, including corn and cotton.

The **Lantern Bug** *(Fulgora lanternaria)*, found in the Amazon rain forest in South America, sometimes is called the peanut bug, because the unusual shape of its head seems to resemble a peanut. It is a member of the lantern-fly family (Fulgoridae). Another form of lantern fly, *Fulgora servillei*, has designs called "pheasant eyes" on its hind wings, which it spreads when in danger, to scare predators. At rest, lantern bugs resemble tree bark. This insect sucks sap from trees, and eats fruits and flower nectar. Other *Fulgora* species live in Asia.

The **Red-Eyed Tree Frog** (*Agalychnis callidryas*), also called monkey frog because of its agility, uses vivid and varied colors for both camouflage and mimicry. It also changes color from green to reddish brown when affected by specific "emotions." The frog's neon-green back and head blend with rain-forest foliage when the protruding red eyes are closed. Hunting at night, this 2"–3" creature sleeps in daytime on the underside of leaves, with bright-orange toepads and thighs tucked away and cream-color belly and throat unseen. To escape predators it shows bright "flash colors" on its flanks. While the predator stares at the startling bright color, the frog leaps away.

5

Pipefish are in the family Syngnathidae, with sea horses and sea dragons. Some species are the **Ornate Ghost Pipefish** and the **Harlequin Ghost Pipefish**. Most species live in warm seas, but a few live in fresh water. Their fringed appendages enable them to blend in with seaweed, eel grass, and sea grass on the ocean floor. They also can change color to match their surroundings. Ranging from 4" to 12" long, they lack a tail fin and swim slowly. Their long, tubular snouts are toothless. Fussy eaters, pipefish may spit out tiny crustaceans they have taken in.

The **Cheetah** (*Acinonyx jubatus*) lives in eastern and southern Africa's savanna grasslands, semidesert areas, bushlands, and open woodlands. A pattern of irregular black spots on its pale brown or tawny yellow coat helps it avoid being seen in the grass or bushes when it stalks prey.

Adult cheetahs may be 4.5' long, plus their long tails. The speediest runners among mammals, cheetahs reach high speeds quickly, but cannot maintain them long. Cheetahs commonly hunt Thomson's gazelles and impalas, often starting a high-speed chase after stalking a herd from cover.

7

An example of the tree-hopper family, Membradicae, is the **Thorn-Mimic Tree Hopper** (*Campylenchia latipes*), found only in California. It is one of several species of tree hopper that mimic thorns. Such varieties are found in many countries. Many species are brightly colored, in dif-

fering patterns. The Thorn-Mimic Tree Hopper, 1/4" long, has a dark reddish-brown head and body, with cinnamon-brown wings and crest. This insect pest sucks sap from trees and shrubs. The female presses her eggs into slits in twigs, which often kills the twigs.

The bottom-dwelling angler-fish species, also known as goose fish and monk fish, are closely related to the frog-fish species, which have various colorings, so that each species is camouflaged in its habitat. The **Sargassum**

Angler Fish (*Histrio histrio*, formerly *Lophius histrio*), named for the seaweed in which it camouflages itself, lives in tropical seas. Like many related species, it has a spiny head, small upturned eyes, a wide mouth, and large teeth.

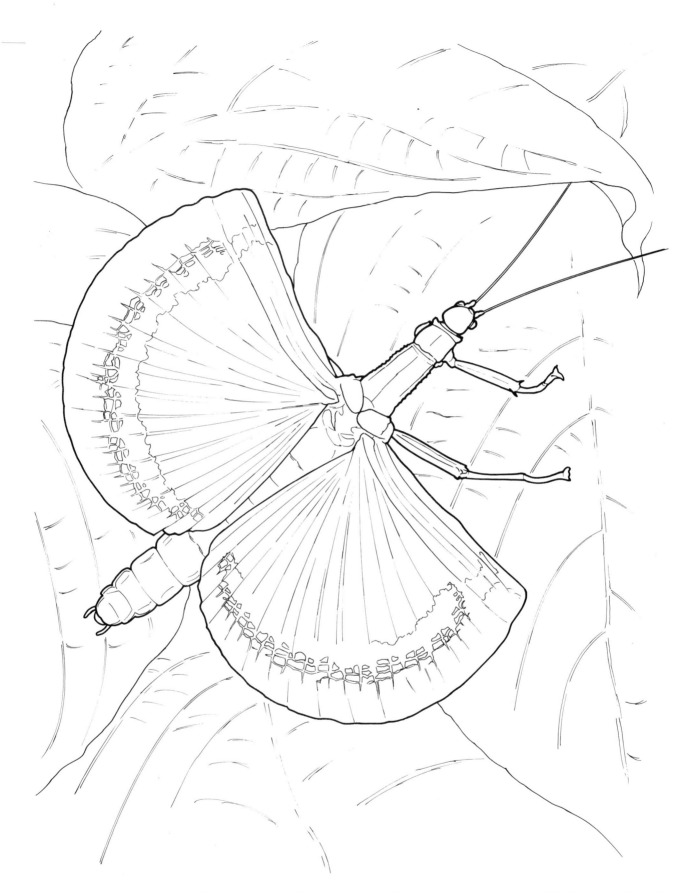

There are many varieties of walkingstick insect found around the world. The species that live in the United States have no wings, but many of the other species do. One species, found in Malaysia, flashes its colorful wings to startle predators. The body and legs of the walkingstick resemble twigs when its wings are folded close to the body, and in the wingless species. The insect may be yellow-green or brown in color. One species, 13" long, is the world's longest insect.

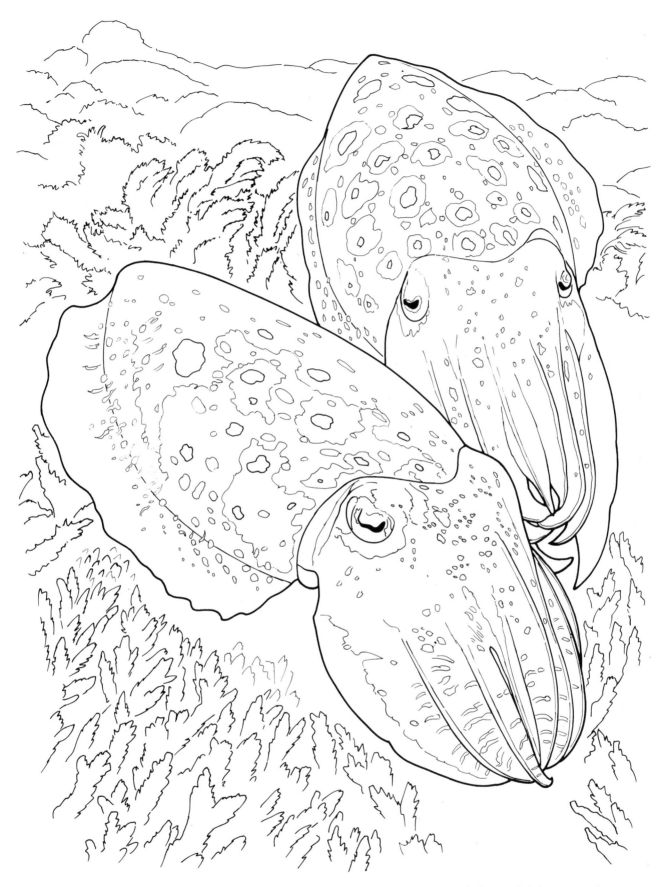

The **Common Cuttlefish** *(Sepia officinalis)*, found in the Atlantic Ocean, the North Sea, and the Mediterranean Sea, can change its mantle's color to match its surroundings in less than a second—much faster than the better-known camouflage artist, the chameleon. Changing skin texture also is part of the cuttlefish's camouflage. Some color changes reflect the cuttlefish's state of excitement, as well. Usually the back is brown to violet and the belly is pale, with blue-green specks. Cuttlefish, like squid, have eight arms and two longer tentacles.

The **Common Walkingstick** or **Northern Walkingstick** (*Diapheromera femorata*), found in the United States east of the Rocky Mountains, is 2" to 3" long. One U.S. species, *Megaphasma dentricus*, at 7" long, is the longest U.S. insect. Far away, a rare giant species is found on the island of Bali. The walkingstick may be green or brown and looks like a twig. Its eggs look like seeds or beans. The six long, jointed legs can lie alongside the body. While the insect feeds on leaves at night, its camouflage protects it from predators.

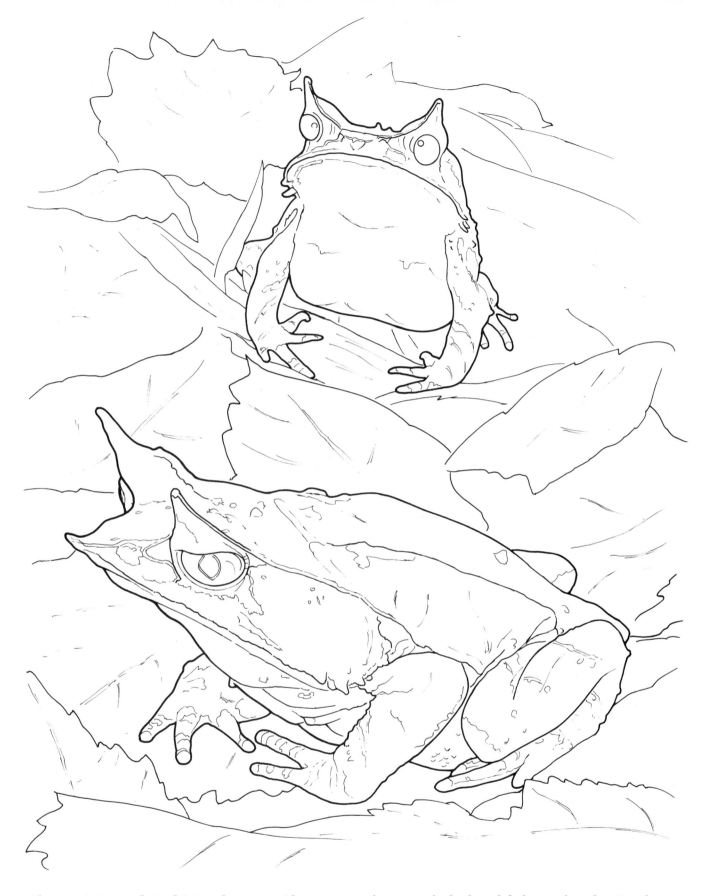

The **Asiatic Horned Toad** (*Megophrys nasuta*) has many different common names, including **Malaysian Horned Toad**. It lives in southeast Asia on the rain-forest floor, where its coloration enables it to camouflage itself in the leaf litter. Its smooth skin is mottled gray, tan, and russet brown on the back, and darker on the sides. Females are about 5" long, but males may be less than half that size. This ferocious toad eats spiders, baby rodents, lizards, and frogs, but it especially likes to eat crabs, and scorpions are its main food.

These East African plant-hopper larvae resemble flowers on plants on which they feed. The insect also has nymph and adult phases. Plant hoppers, in the insect order Homoptera with aphids and cicadas, are pests that pierce plants and suck their juices with mouthparts located on the back of the head. They also inject plants with a digestive fluid. In Africa and Asia, the **Brown Plant Hopper** (*Eumetopina flavipipes*) is a disease vector that destroys rice crops. Larvae of the *Myndus crudus* and *Haplaxius crudus* species host a disease that destroys coconut trees.

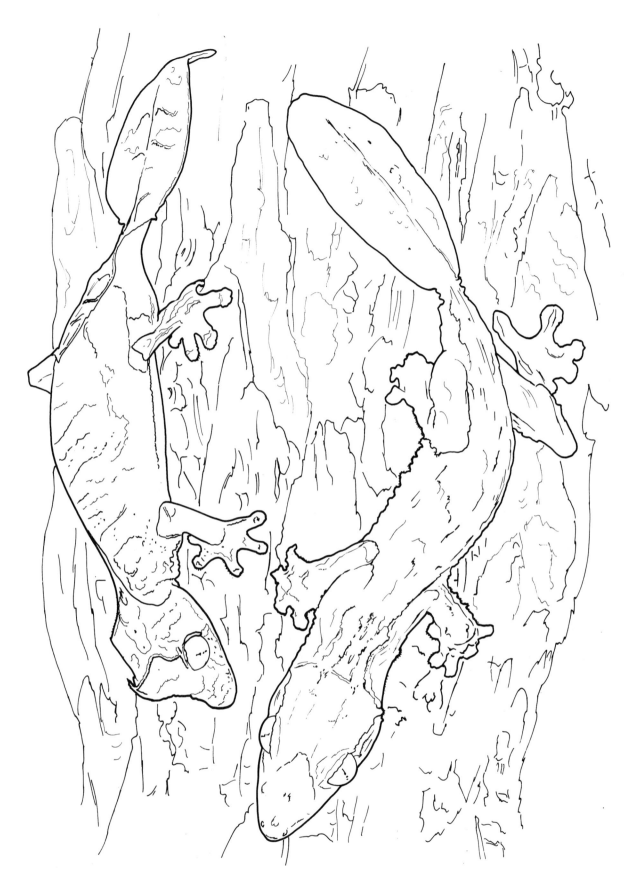

The **Madagascar Spiny Gecko** (*Paroedura bastardi bastardi* and *Paroedura bastardi ibityensis*) can camouflage itself by changing color from light to dark to escape the notice of predators and to enable it to surprise the insects and spiders it hunts at night in the trees where it lives. This gecko also startles predators by shooting out its bright-red tongue. When undisturbed, the Madagascar Spiny Gecko has an olive-green or brownish background color, with paler, dark-edged blotches on it. If caught by its tail, it can escape by dropping the tail; the gecko grows another one later.

The **Arctic Hare** *(Lepus timidus)*, shown in the foreground, has a brown coat on its back in summer, but in winter the all-white hare is camouflaged in the snow. Large feet, like snowshoes used by humans, keep the hare from sinking into the snow. It forages for food at dawn and dusk on the Arctic's rocky slopes and tundra. The **Alpine Snow** **Grouse** *(Lagopus lagopus)*, or **Willow Ptarmigan**, migrates from the Arctic to the U.S. Northwest in winter. Then its feathers are all white, except for a black tail, but in summer the back and wingtops are grayish buff with darker speckles. Found in Japan, Switzerland, and other lands, this bird lives among rocks and sleeps in snow caves.

The 5" **Long-Nosed Hawkfish** (*Oxycirrhites typus*) is a rare inhabitant of deep water around reefs in various parts of the Pacific Ocean, including the waters near the Philippines, Indonesia, Hawaii, and Mexico's Baja California peninsula. The Hawkfish remains motionless in its habitat, where the camouflage pattern on its body enables it to blend in with its surroundings. Its flexible dorsal-fin rays and its dorsal spines with tiny threadlike trailers at their tips also help it to remain unseen among branched coral.

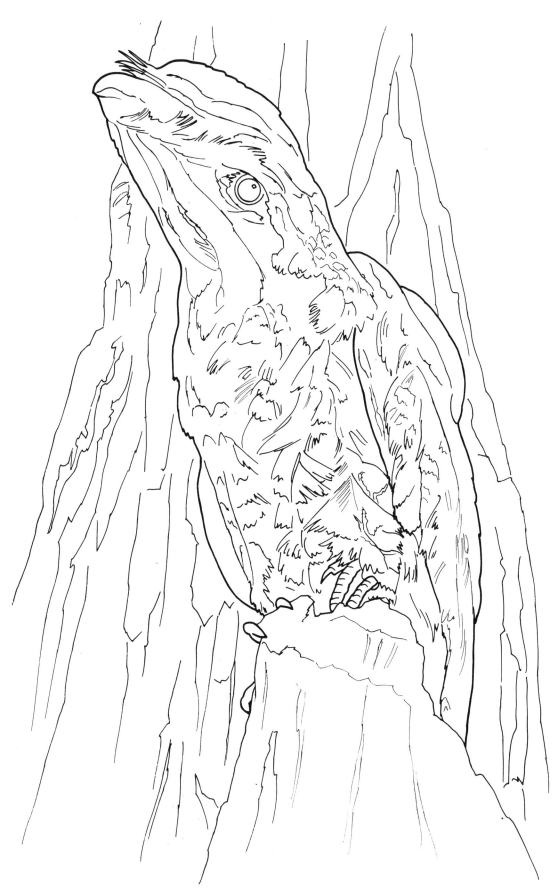

Found in New Guinea (north of Australia), in the Solomon Islands, and in northeast Australia, the **Papuan Frogmouth** *(Podargus papuensis)* is a nocturnal bird that rests on the trunks of giant rain-forest trees, blending in with the bark because of its mottled coloration. When disturbed, it opens its big mouth to scare predators. Related species are the **Marbled Frogmouth** *(Podargus ocellatus)* and the **Tawny Frogmouth** *(Podargus strigoides)*.

This moth's mottled pattern of brown and orange coloration enables it to remain unseen as it rests on the bark of a tree in Costa Rica. The moth is a member of the Saturniidae family. Among the Saturniidae, *Eacles*, *Hylesia*, and *Lonomia* species are found in Central America. Africa is home to many species of this family.

African Flower Mantises, which have markings that enable them to blend in very well with the flowers around them, usually hang from a branch, head down and motionless, swaying in the breeze, when they shed their skin. The young of *Hymenopus bicornis* resemble blossoms of various colors. The **Orchid Mantis,** about 2.5" long, lives in the rain forest. It has petal-like leg flaps and spiny forelegs.

The rare **Leafy Sea Dragon** (*Phycodurus eques*), unique to Australia's south coast, lives on the weedy sea bottom or in kelp forests, near reefs, in cold water. About 18" long and toothless, it is closely related to the much more common **Weedy Sea Dragon** or **Common Sea Dragon**.

Both resemble the underwater vegetation in which they live. The Leafy Sea Dragon changes color from yellow, pink, and orange to seaweed brown. Also, males change color rapidly during courtship. These creatures mimic sea grass swayed by underwater currents.

The foot-long **Panther Chameleon** (*Pardalis furcifer*) lives in hot, humid rain forests on the coasts of Madagascar. It changes color to communicate (for example, anger and sexual excitement) as well as to camouflage itself from both predators and prey. Males are dark green, with pale blue bands along each side, but the green changes to reds and yellows when the reptile is sexually aroused or aggressive. Panther chameleons are hunted by lemurs (also unique to Madagascar), snakes, and birds. They eat insects. **Parson's Chameleon** (*Chamaeleo parsonii*) also lives in east Madagascar and eats insects. Nearly 2' long, it has rough skin and is the heaviest chameleon.

Octopuses are mollusks, in the class Cephalopoda (this Latin word indicates that the "feet" or tentacles grow out of the creature's head) and the order Octopoda (this Latin word means "eight feet"). They live in undersea rock crevices and can squeeze their soft bodies through very narrow spaces. All octopuses camouflage themselves by changing color to match their surroundings. On sandy bottoms in Indonesia's waters live recently discovered **Mimic Octopus** varieties (*Octopus* species), which change color, texture, shape, body position, and movement modes to imitate sea creatures (some of which are venomous) as diverse as flounders, sea snakes, jellyfish, stingrays, and sea horses.

Many **Hermit Crab** species, members of the family Pauridae, live in the empty shells of dead sea snails and other gastropod mollusks. The hermit crab *Petrochirus diogenes* carries **Cloak Anemones** *(Calliactis tricolor)* and other species of sea anemone on its conch-shell shelter, as camouflage to protect it from predators (large fish). Sea anemones are animals that somewhat resemble underwater flowers. Their stinging tentacles are additional protection for the hermit crabs.

The **Tawny Owl** (*Strix aluco*), also called hoot owl, screech owl, and many other names, is the most common owl in Europe. It hunts at night in the woods, where its coloration helps it blend in with the trees. It eats small mammals, birds, and fish. Most of this owl's feathers are chestnut brown, streaked with buff, black, and white. The breast feathers are buff with black or brown markings, and this owl has buff-colored "eyebrows."

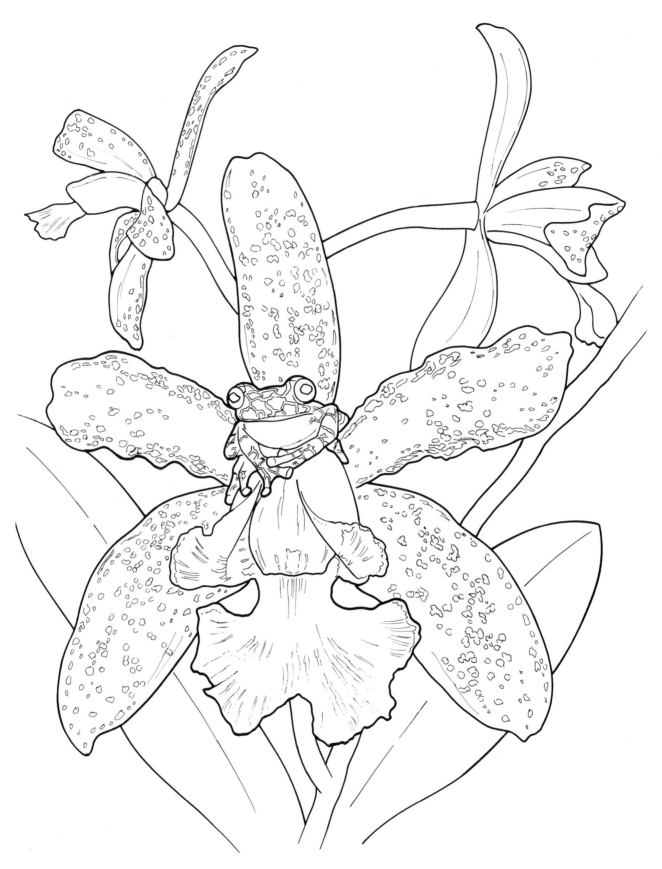

This tree frog's colors and markings blend with the yellow-green speckled with red-brown *Cattleya Aclandiae* orchid, its perch. Although very few of the world's plants have green flowers, six *Cattleya* orchid species found in Brazil have petals and sepals that are some shade of green. The flowers also have crimson, magenta, purple, or red-brown spots at the lip. Tree frogs (about 600 species) may be ash-white, tan, yellow, green, red, brown, black, or gray, with various markings. Diverse coloration of both orchids and frogs makes many camouflage pairings possible.

The flower of the **Bee Orchid** (*Ophrys apifera*) resembles a female **Long-Horn Bee** (*Eucera longicornis*) and even has a perfume that smells like those bees. Male *Eucera* bees, which live in areas from central Europe to North Africa, are attracted to the flowers and pollinate them. The lip of the orchid flower has five lobes and is red-brown or dark purple. Other species in the *Ophrys* genus, such as the **Fly Orchid** (*Ophrys insectifera*) also have flowers that resemble the female of some insect species.

The **Palm Viper** or **Palm Pit Viper** (*Bothriechis nigroviridis),* found in Central America (Costa Rica) and Panama, is green, spotted with black on the head and back. It mainly hunts in the evening and at night. During the day, when it hangs in trees by its prehensile tail, its cam- ouflage coloration keeps it unseen. It bites plantation workers when disturbed. This golden-eyed snake averages 30" in length. The various pit-viper species are named for heat-sensing pits between each eye and nostril, which detect the presence of warm-blooded animals in the dark.